W9-BNJ-089

A Taste of culture

Foods of Chile

Barbara Sheen

KIDHAVEN PRESS
A part of Gale, Cengage Learning

GALE
CENGAGE Learning

Detroit • New York • San Francisco • New Haven, Conn • Waterville, Maine • London

GALE
CENGAGE Learning™

LIBRARY OF CONGRESS CATALOGING-IN-PUBLICATION DATA

Sheen, Barbara.
  Foods of Chile / by Barbara Sheen.
       p. cm. -- (A taste of culture)
  Includes bibliographical references and index.
  ISBN 978-0-7377-5421-6 (hardcover)
  1. Cooking, Chilean--Juvenile literature. 2. Cookbooks. I. Title.
  TX716.C5S55 2010
  641.5983--dc22

                                                                2010035995

Kidhaven Press
27500 Drake Rd.
Farmington Hills MI 48331

ISBN-13: 978-0-7377-5421-6
ISBN-10: 0-7377-5421-4

Printed in the United States of America
1 2 3 4 5 6 7 14 13 12 11 10

Printed by Bang Printing, Brainerd, MN, 1st Ptg., 12/2010

Contents

A Land of Plenty

When the Spanish **conquistador** (con-KEY-sta-dor) Pedro Valdivia arrived in Chile's central valley in 1541 looking for riches, he sent a letter to King Phillip II of Spain describing the landscape he saw. In it he wrote, "This land is such that life here cannot be equaled. It is abundant in grass, and can support any kind of cattle or livestock and plants that you can imagine. ... It seems that God has created everything [here]."[1]

Chile has always been a land of plenty. Located on the tip of South America, nestled between the Andes Mountains in the east and the Pacific Ocean in the west, Chile is the longest and narrowest country in the world.

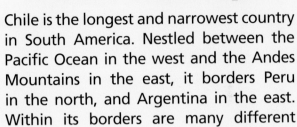

Chilean Landscapes

Chile is the longest and narrowest country in South America. Nestled between the Pacific Ocean in the west and the Andes Mountains in the east, it borders Peru in the north, and Argentina in the east.

Within its borders are many different landscapes. In the north is the Atacama (Ah-ta-CAH-ma) desert. It is the world's driest desert. Calama, a town in the desert, is the driest town in the world because it has never rained here.

Central Chile has fertile valleys. Santiago, the nation's capital is located in central Chile. Southern Chile features rich grazing land, forests, and many volcanoes and lakes. The southernmost part of Chile, known as Patagonia (Pah-tah-GO-nee-ah), contains glaciers, icebergs, and islands. Among these is an archipelago, or string of islands, known as Tierra del Fuego (tee-AIR-a del foo-AY-go). Temperatures rival those of Antarctica, and penguins outnumber people in Tierra del Fuego.

It is blessed with a varied geography and climate, fertile soil, rich grazing land, 2,647 miles (4,270km) of coastline, and a clean environment. This winning combination provides the Chilean people with a huge variety of fresh local foods. Seafood, corn, avocados, and beans are among their favorites.

Fish and Shellfish

Chileans love seafood, and there is plenty of it in Chile. Since Chile is only about 110 miles (177km) wide, no place in Chile is far from the ocean. The Humboldt

Chilean markets overflow with freshly caught seafood, which is a staple of the Chilean diet.

Current, a cold, nutrient-rich area of water where marine life thrives, flows off the coast of Chile. It provides the Chilean people with a staggering abundance of fresh seafood.

Fishing has been a part of Chilean life since 12000 BC when migrating tribes first settled in Chile. Today, fishing is a major Chilean industry. Chile is a leading exporter of sea bass, abalone, and salmon that is raised on special farms.

At home, fresh seafood is available on almost every dock and beach along Chile's long coast. Fishermen slice and sell their catch right off their boats. A few steps away, little seaside cafés serve up fish that were still swimming a few hours earlier.

Chilean markets overflow with freshly caught seafood. In the Central Market of Santiago (sahn-tee-AH-go), Chile's capital, rows of seafood vendors offer tons of fresh fish and shellfish. "If it swims, it is here,"[2] Travel Channel host Andrew Zimmern says. There are clams, oysters, shrimp, lobster, scallops, eels, mussels, crabs, octopuses, swordfish, and squid, to name just a few, all freshly caught that same day.

More than sixty informal eateries known as **picadas** (pee-CAH-dahs) dot the market. They are almost always crowded with hungry Chileans. Grilled sea bass, clams cooked in lemon juice, baked scallops topped with parmesan cheese, raw oysters, and crispy batter-fried eel, are just a few of the fresh choices. Many Chileans head to the picadas first thing in the morning for a breakfast of mariscal (MAR-ee-scahl), a garlicky chowder brimming over with every type of shellfish imaginable.

Corn

Chile is also one of the world's leading producers of fruits and vegetables. Many of the fruits and vegetables sold in North America during the winter come from Chile, which is located in the Southern Hemisphere, where the seasons are reversed from those in the Northern Hemisphere. Like Chilean fish markets, the country's produce markets offer an astounding variety of freshly picked fruits and vegetables such as mangoes, papayas, figs, strawberries, grapes, peppers, squash, pumpkins, onions, avocados, tomatoes, olives, potatoes, and corn.

Chili Peppers in Chilean Cooking

Some people think that the nation of Chile got its name because Chilean cooking contains lots of chili peppers, which makes Chilean foods very hot and spicy. These people are wrong. Chile is not named for hot peppers. The name comes from a Mapuche Indian word that describes the snow-capped Andes Mountains. In reality, chili peppers are rarely used in Chilean main dishes and Chilean cooking is not very spicy.

The peppers are used, however, to make pebre (PAY-bray), a dipping sauce that is served with bread at the start of almost every meal. There are many different ways to make pebre. Most include a green pepper known as ají verde (ah-HEE VAYR-day), tomatoes, garlic, onions, lemon juice, and cilantro.

Contrary to popular belief, chile peppers are rarely used in Chilean main dishes and are not the source of the country's name.

Chilean cooks make good use of all these delicious foods. Corn, in particular, is very popular. Corn is native to Chile. Chileans have been eating it for thousands of years. It was a vital part of the diet of Chile's native people. They cooked it with beans, pumpkins, and tomatoes—a nutritious combination that provides a good balance of proteins and vitamins.

Corn is still an important part of the Chilean peo-

Corn and Green Bean Salad

This popular Chilean side dish combines two popular foods—corn and beans. It is easy to make. Fresh or frozen vegetables can be used.

Ingredients
2 cups cooked green beans
1 cup cooked corn kernels
¼ cup mayonnaise
1 teaspoon mustard
⅓ red bell pepper, chopped
1 teaspoon lime juice
salt and pepper to taste

Directions
1. Put the vegetables in a large bowl.
2. Mix mayonnaise, mustard, and lime juice together. Add the mixture to the vegetables. Mix well. Add salt and pepper to taste.

Serves 4.

ple's diet. They eat it grilled, toasted, dried, baked, and boiled. They turn it into pies, breads, and casseroles. They add it to soups and stews. They put it in salads. They turn it into a thick, creamy sauce known as pilco (PEEL-co) that they pour on meats. "Corn," explains author Daniel Joelson, "plays a versatile [multipurpose] role in the Chilean kitchen, which uses it in far more dishes than do most countries."[3]

Corn is so popular that many Chileans grow different varieties of the vegetable in their backyards. Sweet corn, pie corn, and white corn are favorites. Bright-yellow sweet corn is perfect for corn on the cob, a popular Chilean snack. Pie corn has wide yellow kernels that Chileans grind into a thick paste that is the basis for savory pies and casseroles. White corn has even larger kernels. Each kernel is about the size of a penny. Chilean cooks use the white kernels in pies, casseroles, soups, and salads.

Avocados

Avocados are another favorite native food. Their skin, which is not to be eaten, is greenish black. Their flesh is light green. The flesh is hard when the fruit is first picked, but it softens to a butter-like texture. The fruit is harvested year-round. Huge avocado trees grow in Chilean parks and gardens. These evergreen trees can grow up to 80 feet (24.38m) tall.

Avocado farming is also big business. Chile is one of the world's leading growers and exporters of the creamy fruit, and a leading consumer of it. Chileans spread mashed avocados seasoned with salt and pepper on anything and everything. Susan Kohen, who grew

Avocado farming is a large business in Chile that provides locals with a favorite native food.

Palta Reina

Palta reina is not difficult to make. It is a good light meal for a hot day.

Ingredients
2 large, firm ripe avocados
1 chicken breast, cooked and shredded
¼ cup mayonnaise
4 pitted black olives
1 tablespoon chopped tomato
1 tablespoon chopped green onion
4 large lettuce leaves
½ lemon
salt and pepper to taste

Directions
1. Cut the avocados in half lengthwise. Remove the pits. Squeeze a little lemon juice on each avocado section.
2. In a bowl combine the chicken, tomatoes, green onion, mayonnaise, and salt and pepper.
3. Get four plates. Put one lettuce leaf on each plate. Put an avocado half on each leaf. Fill each avocado half with the chicken mixture. Top each with an olive.

Serves 4.

up in Chile, recalls, "My family always had a bag of eight to ten avocados. We would mash them up with tomatoes and salt and put them on sandwiches with cold cuts [assorted sliced meat]."[4] This spread is so popular that fast-food restaurants throughout Chile provide canisters of mashed avocado beside those of mustard and ketchup.

Avocados also accompany meat and fish and are a popular addition to salads. They are the main ingredient in palta reina (PAHL-ta ray-EE-na), or queen avocado. This popular Chilean dish consists of a pitted avocado half stuffed with chicken or fish salad and topped with an olive, which looks like the queen's crown.

As Chilean as Beans

Beans, too, accompany most meals, and have been part of Chilean life for centuries. Beans were an important part of Chile's native people's diet, and have long been a campfire staple of Chilean **huasos** (oo-AH-sohs), or cowboys.

A creamy bowl of beans accompanied by pickled vegetables is a popular first course in Chile. Beans are featured in soups, stews, and salads. Beans are so much a part of Chilean culture that the saying "He is as Chilean as beans" is a common way for Chileans to describe each other.

Chilean markets overflow with baskets of beans in every shape, size, and color. There are white beans, speckled red beans, plump garbanzo beans, tiny grey turtle beans, and spotted purple cranberry beans, to name a few. The beans may be fresh or dried. In most countries, beans are dried so that they can be stored and eaten in the winter. In Chile, fresh beans are available year-round. They are a popular favorite.

Fresh beans are more difficult to prepare than dried beans. Before they can be cooked, they must be shelled and carefully skinned. But the results are worth the effort. Fresh beans have a clean, pure taste that Chileans love.

A variety of beans accompany most Chilean meals. The markets are filled with beans of every color, shape, and size.

"Chileans," author Ruth Van Waerebeek-Gonzalez explains, "are passionate about their beans. Winter or summer, rich or poor, from the country folks to the urban Santiaguinos [residents of Santiago, Chile], everyone has a soft spot for a satisfying bowl of beans."[5]

On any given day, Chileans can find dozens of varieties of beans to satisfy their passion. Chilean markets overflow with an awesome selection of fresh foods. Although Chilean cooks have many foods to choose from, fresh fish and shellfish, brightly colored beans, creamy avocados, and long ears of corn hold a special place in their kitchens. These fresh, tasty ingredients are a part of Chilean life and history.

chapter 2

A Cultural Exchange

Chile was first settled around 12000 BC by migrating groups who historians say came from either Asia or Polynesia, a group of islands in the South Pacific. Chile's first people relied on seafood, wild game, and native plants like corn, squash, potatoes, peppers, avocados, and tomatoes for food.

In 1541 Pedro de Valdivia came to Chile. He founded the city of Santiago, which became the nation's capital. Spanish settlers followed. They were amazed at the variety of foods they found in Chile, many of which they had never seen before. They brought other foodstuff with them, which were new to Chile's native people. Over time, the two groups adopted each other's foods and cooking styles. The Chilean people's favorite dishes

The Mapuche Indians

The Mapuche (mah-POO-chay) Indians, who made their home in southern Chile, were the only native group in South America that could not be conquered by the Spaniards. After repeated battles with the Mapuche people, in 1641 the King of Spain signed a treaty recognizing the Mapuche people and the territory they inhabited as an independent nation called Araucania (Ah-rah-ooh-CAHN-ee-ah).

The Mapuche lived as a self-governing nation for two centuries. After Chile gained its independence from Spain, it broke the Spanish treaty with the Mapuche people and began occupying parts of Araucania. By the end of the 19th century, Chile had taken over Araucania.

Today there are an estimated 1 million Mapuche people in Chile, many of whom live in Santiago. They have retained their native language and culture, and are working to legally regain Araucania.

reflect this cultural exchange.

The National Dish

Pastel de choclo (pah-STEHL day CHO-clo) is Chile's national dish. It combines native and Spanish ingredients in a sweet and savory pie. Pastel de choclo consists of a mixture of ground beef and onion known as **pino** (PEE-no), baked with chicken, hard-boiled eggs, olives, and raisins, topped with a corn and sugar crust.

The Spanish introduced cattle, chickens, pork, olives, sugar, and other foods to Chile. Before their arrival, Chile's native people's main source of meat was

Pictured is Chile's national dish, pastel de choclo. It combines ground beef, onion, chicken, hard-boiled eggs, raisins, and olives with a sugar and corn crust to make a sweet and savory pie.

guanaco (gwah-NAH-co), a llama-like animal native to the Andes. That changed with the introduction of beef and chicken. What did not change was the popularity of corn, which was a new food for the Spanish. In fact, the corn topping on pastel de choclo is similar to toppings found in many dishes created by the **Mapuche** (mah-POO-chay). The Mapuche are the native people who settled in southern Chile.

Not just any corn will do when preparing pastel de choclo. Only large kernel white corn is used. It has a

All in the Same Family

When people think of camels, they rarely think of Chile. But four animals that are natives of Chile—llamas, alpacas, guanacos, and vicuñas—are members of the camel family. These animals have long necks, small heads, and wooly coats.

Llamas are the largest animals of the group. They can weigh up to 300 pounds (136kg). Llamas are intelligent and gentle. Historians think they are the oldest domesticated animals on Earth. They have been used as pack animals in Chile for at least 4,000 years.

Alpacas also have been domesticated. They are raised for their extremely soft wool, which comes in 22 colors. Alpacas are about one-third the size of llamas.

Guanacos and vicuñas are wild animals that live in herds. Guanacos are larger than alpacas, but smaller than llamas. Vicuñas are the smallest of all.

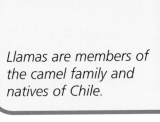
Llamas are members of the camel family and natives of Chile.

creamy texture. To make the topping, Chilean cooks mix the corn with sugar, butter, eggs, and milk. They fry ground beef with onions and garlic for the filling. They cook the chicken in boiling water with herbs, and they hard-boil the eggs.

When the filling is done, they layer it in a traditional red clay pan, which adds color and an earthy taste to the pie. First comes the pino, next the chicken, and finally the raisins, olives, and hard-boiled eggs. The whole thing is topped with the corn mix and sprinkled with sugar.

The idea of combining sweet and savory flavors was brought to Spain by the **Moors**, the North African people who occupied Spain for 800 years. The Spanish brought it to Chile. Corn, with its sweet and salty taste, was a perfect addition to Moorish recipes. The result is a delicious dish that, according to Ruth Van Waerebeek-Gonzalez, is "a perfect example of the interaction between the cuisines [foods] of the Spanish conquistadors and the indigenous [native] Mapuche population."[6]

A Chilean Clambake

Curanto (coo-RAHN-toe), which means "hot stones" in the Mapuche language, is the Chilean version of a clambake. It combines native and Spanish ingredients with the ancient Mapuche practice of cooking food in a pit filled with hot stones.

Preparing curanto is quite time consuming, which may be why on the southern Chilean island of Chiloé

Curanto—the Chilean version of a clambake—is traditionally a communal celebration that involves a great deal of food and lasts all day.

Caldillo de Congrio

This fish chowder has lots of ingredients, but it is not hard to make. Chilean congrio (an eel-like fish) is hard to find in North America. This recipe uses cod instead. Any firm white fish, or salmon, will work well.

Ingredients
1 pound of cod filet, cut into chunks
1 medium onion, chopped
2 garlic cloves, chopped
1 carrot, peeled and cut in chunks
4 small tomatoes, chopped
3 tablespoons olive oil
3 cups clam juice mixed with 2 cups water
1 cup cream
1 can baby potatoes
1 jalapeño pepper, seeds and veins removed, chopped
¼ teaspoon oregano
salt and pepper to taste

(chee-lo-AY) making and eating curanto is, traditionally, a communal celebration that lasts a whole day and involves mountains of food and lots of people.

First a large pit is dug. It is partially filled with stones. A wood fire is lit on top of the stones. Its purpose is to heat the stones, which takes a few hours. When the stones are blistering hot, they are covered with large seaweed leaves. Then, the food is layered on top of the leaves. Originally, the ingredients consisted of shellfish, potatoes, corn, and seasonal vegetables. After the

Directions

1. Heat the oil in a large stockpot. Add the onions, garlic, jalapeño, and carrot. Cook over low heat until the vegetables are soft.
2. Add the tomatoes, oregano, potatoes, and clam juice. Cook over low heat until the soup boils.
3. Add the fish. Cover and cook over low heat about 20 minutes, or until the fish is cooked.
4. Mix in the cream and salt and pepper to taste.

Serve with crusty bread and lemon wedges. Serves 4–6.

Caldillo de Congrio contains native vegetables and chunks of congrio, which is difficult to find in North America.

arrival of the Spanish, chicken, sausage, and pork were added to the mix.

A layer of seaweed separates each ingredient. The whole thing is topped with a damp piece of burlap cloth. The leaves and damp cloth keep the steam in and the food moist. The food cooks for about an hour and then it is ready to eat.

Because preparing curanto in this traditional manner requires so much time and effort, many modern Chileans make a similar dish on their stovetop. This home version features the same ingredients, but fennel or cabbage leaves are used to separate each layer.

Whether cooked in the ground or on the stove, curanto is usually served with fish broth and potato bread. The dish is very rich and filling, with an earthy aroma and a hearty flavor. It is a perfect dish for the cold, wet southern part of Chile where eating it is a centuries' old tradition.

"The Essence of Chile"

Caldillo de congrio (cal-DEE-yo day con-GREE-oh), or conger chowder, is another popular dish that Chileans have been eating for centuries. It features congrio, a long, thin, white sea creature that looks like an eel but is actually a fish. Chileans consider congrio a delicacy.

Caldillo de congrio is a popular Chilean dish. It features congrio, an eel-like fish, which is melded with vegetables and other flavors to make a fish chowder.

They call it the "King of Fish," and love its sweet taste and firm texture.

The chowder starts with a broth made from the fish's head and bones. Chunks of congrio and native vegetables such as potatoes, tomatoes, carrots, garlic,

Charquicán

Charquicán can be made with dried or fresh beef. Different vegetables may be added or subtracted from the recipe, depending on taste. Corn, potatoes, carrots, and pumpkin are almost always included.

Ingredients
1 pound beef cut into strips
1 large carrot, peeled and cut into small chunks
2 medium potatoes, peeled and cut into small chunks
¼ pound pumpkin, peeled, cut into chunks
1 small onion, chopped
2 cloves garlic chopped
1 cup frozen corn
¼ cup beef or chicken broth
3 tablespoons olive oil
salt and pepper to taste

Instructions
1. Heat the oil in a pan over medium heat.
2. Add the meat, onion, potatoes, pumpkin, corn, carrots, and garlic.
3. Cook for about 10 minutes.
4. Add the broth and salt and pepper to taste. Cook on low heat until the liquid is absorbed; about 20 minutes.

Serves 4.

bell peppers, and onions are cooked in the broth. Often shrimp, mussels, or scallops are added, too. When all the flavors have melded together, cream is added to the chowder, which is the Spaniards' contribution to the recipe. The cream makes the soup rich and velvety.

The soup tastes and smells of both the ocean and the earth. It is so beloved in Chile that Pablo Neruda, a famous Chilean poet who won the Nobel Prize in Literature in 1971, wrote a poem in honor of the dish. In it he calls caldillo de congrio "the essence [heart] of Chile … [in which] the tastes from sea and land arrive newly wed to the table."[7]

Chilean Beef Stew

Charquicán (char-coo-ee-CAHN), a delicious stew, is another Chilean favorite. It combines beef with the native vegetables that Chile's first people depended on. At first, Chilean Indians used guanaco meat for the stew. They cut the meat into thin strips and air-dried it much like jerky before slowly cooking it with potatoes, beans, corn, squash, peppers, and carrots. Drying the meat was a good way to preserve it. Slow cooking helped to tenderize it. Once the Spanish arrived with cattle and horses, dried beef or dried horsemeat was substituted for guanaco.

Today, Chile is home to many large cattle ranches. Fresh beef is so plentiful in Chile that drying beef is no lon-

Cochayuyo (pictured) is a popular type of dried seaweed used in Chilean cooking.

ger necessary. Instead fresh meat, which is still slowly cooked with a great variety of fresh vegetables, is used. Most cooks do not follow a set recipe, but rather throw whatever vegetables are in season into the pot. Some cooks add cochayuyo (co-cha-YOO-yo), a type of dried seaweed that is popular in Chile. Vegetarians often substitute it for beef. It has a meaty flavor and, like beef, it is loaded with protein.

The end result is a thick, hearty, and colorful stew that reminds Chileans of their history and their home. "Food brings you back to your loved ones, your home, your siblings, it is related to your roots and

your love for your land," says Cecilia Fernandez, a Chilean cook. "If I eat charquicán it tells me about my birth, home, mother, my smells."[8]

Chile's favorite dishes all remind Chileans of their history, of their Indian and Spanish ancestors, and of the cultural exchange that created Chilean cooking.

Tea Time

Tea time, or **onces** (OWN-says), is snack time in Chile. Chileans inherited the practice of taking a tea break from English immigrants who settled in Chile in the 18th century. Some of these immigrants ran Chilean mines. Following English tradition, they allowed their employees to take a tea break in the late afternoon. During this break many of the miners drank a type of whiskey called aguardiente (ahg-WAHR-dee-EN-tay), which means "firewater" in English. Not wanting their bosses to know they were drinking alcohol, the miners referred to the break as *once* (OWN-say), the Spanish word for eleven, which is the number of letters in the word aguardiente. Modern Chileans also take their tea

break in the late afternoon or early evening and, although they are not likely to drink aguardiente during this time, they still refer to tea time as *onces*.

Most Chileans eat supper at 9 or 10 P.M. Onces, which can be a cup of tea and a light meal or tea and a sweet treat, serve as a way to tide them over until suppertime. It is also a time for friends to get together and socialize. "When I grew up," Kohen recalls, "we had four meals a day: breakfast, a big lunch, tea time at about five, and then a light dinner. People still eat tea called 'onces' and then a light dinner. When ladies socialize they do it at onces or tea time."[9]

Lots of Sandwiches

Sandwiches are a popular onces treat. Chileans love big, thick, hot sandwiches covered with colorful toppings. In fact, Chilean sandwiches are so fat and juicy that they must be eaten with a knife and fork. "It's not

Chilean Earthquakes

Large earthquakes seem to occur in Chile every 25 to 100 years. Two sections of the Earth's crust, called the South American and the Nazca plates, meet under Chile. These plates move. If they bump into each other, the result is an earthquake.

In 1960 and 2010, two of the largest earthquakes ever recorded occurred in Chile. The 1960 earthquake was the strongest earthquake in history. It measured 9.5 on the Richter scale, a tool used to measure the strength of an earthquake. The earthquake caused landslides that changed the course of rivers and dammed some rivers up, creating new lakes in Chile. It caused tsunamis (powerful waves) that reached as far as Hawaii.

The 2010 earthquake measured 8.8. It killed over 500 people, damaged about 500,000 homes, and caused power outages and fires. It also caused tsunamis along Chile's coast.

possible to use your hands, it would surely end on a gastronomic [food-related] disaster, getting dirty. Chilean sandwiches are the biggest ones I've ever seen,"[10] says Margaret Snooks, a writer who lives in Chile.

There are many different types of sandwiches to choose from. Some have interesting names. There is the Barros Luco (BAH-rohs LOO-co), which is made of grilled steak and melted cheese piled on a fluffy freshly baked white bun. It is named after former Chilean president Ramón Barros Luco, who ate the sandwich almost every day. His cousin, Chilean foreign minister

The Barros Jarpa, a grilled ham and cheese sandwich, got its name from Chilean foreign minister Ernesto Barros Jarpa who often ate the sandwich.

Ernesto Barros Jarpa (BAH-rohs HAR-pah), often dined with the president. He preferred ham to steak, which is how the grilled ham-and-cheese sandwich called Barros Jarpa got its name.

Lomitos (lo-MEE-toes) are another favorite sandwich. These sandwiches are made with pork that has been marinated in aromatic spices for hours then browned on a sizzling griddle. The meat is cut into thin slices and placed in a pot of thick, rich broth, which keeps it hot and moist until it is heaped onto a big freshly baked bun. A typical lomito contains about one-half pound (200g) of meat and is a whopping 6 inches (24cm) high. The sandwich, according to Travel Channel host Anthony Bourdain, is "a towering monument. ... [It is] delicious, porktastic."[11]

If these or any other sandwiches are topped with mayonnaise, mashed avocado, and tomato, they become Italianos (ee-TAHL-ee-AH-nos), or Italians, because the colors of the toppings match the colors of the Italian flag. When hot sauce, garlic, and string beans are added to the Italiano, the sandwich becomes a

Chilean Islands

A number of interesting islands are part of Chile. Chiloé Island is the closest to the mainland. It is the home of many little towns and a national park. Blue whales, dolphins, sea lions, and penguins are native to the island and its waters.

Robinson Crusoe Island is farther south. Pirates used it as a hideout in the 17th century. It was also the home of Alexander Selkirk, a marooned sailor whose true-life adventure inspired the book *Robinson Crusoe*.

Another island, named Tierra del Fuego, is separated from mainland Chile by a narrow waterway called the Strait of Magellan. Tierra del Fuego was discovered by Fernando Magellan in 1520, and is located close to Antarctica. The island is rich in oil.

Easter Island is the farthest away. It is located in the southeastern Pacific Ocean about 2,180 miles (3,510km) from Chile. Easter Island is famous for its huge, ancient statues called Moais.

chancarero (chan-ca-RAY-ro), one of the most popular sandwiches in the country. So, a lomito topped with mayonnaise, avocado, and tomato is known as a lomito Italiano, and if hot sauce, garlic, and string beans are also added it is a lomito chancarero.

Giant Hot Dogs

Hot dogs known as **completos** (com-PLAY-toes) are another wildly popular Chilean sandwich. Completos are by no means ordinary hot dogs. Each completo starts with a whopping 1-foot-long (0.30m) hot dog nestled inside an extra-large bun.

The hot dog is just the beginning. Mounds of mashed avocado, sauerkraut, pickled vegetables, onions, tomatoes, and mayonnaise are heaped on top. Although the combination of all these toppings may not sound appealing, the flavors all blend together well without overpowering the taste of the meat. According to Andrew Zimmern, "It's the toppings that make it a rich fattening treat, avocado, tomato, mayonnaise, salad, with onion, and cilantro. … I never would have thought I would like a hot dog with avocado and … mayonnaise on it, but that's really, really good."[12]

The Sweeter, the Better

Sweets made with **manjar** (mahn-HAR), delicious caramel cream that means "delicacy" in Spanish, are another favorite onces treat. Manjar is made with milk and sugar that are slowly simmered until a thick, very sweet toffee-colored paste forms. Manjar, is known

Completos

Chilean completos are loaded with toppings. Feel free to add or subtract toppings to suit your taste.

Ingredients
2 hot dogs, cooked
2 hot dog buns
1 small avocado cut in half, pit removed
1 teaspoon mayonnaise
1 teaspoon chopped onion
1 teaspoon chopped tomato
1 tablespoon sauerkraut
mustard to taste

Directions
1. Spread mustard on the bottom half of the hot dog buns.
2. Scoop out the avocado and mash it in a bowl.
3. Top each hot dog with half of the avocado, onions, sauerkraut, tomatoes, and the mayonnaise. Top with bun tops.
Serves 2.

Chilean completos are often loaded with mashed avocado, sauerkraut, onions, tomatoes, and mayonnaise.

Manjar, known as dulce de leche in Spain, is a caramel cream that is a favorite among Chileans.

as dulce de leche (DOOL-say day LAY-chay) in Spain. Spanish nuns, who came to Chile in the 17th century, created delicious pastries filled with the cream.

Modern Chilean bakers adopted the nuns' recipes. They fill sandwich cookies, layer cakes, and pastries with manjar. They roll sponge cake and delicate pancakes around it. They stuff doughnuts, known as Berlins, with it. Manjar-filled treats are sold in bakeries and cafés, and on busy road sides where local women dressed in white offer homemade treats to commuters. "Vendors of these pastries pop up everywhere in sight," says Joelson. "What a cheerful sight for tired eyes they are when waiting at the tollbooth on the highway."[13]

Besides using manjar to fill pastries, Chileans like to spread it on bread and crackers, much like Americans do peanut butter. Like peanut butter, dozens of brands of manjar are sold ready-made in Chilean supermarkets.

Fruit Treats

Fresh fruit abounds in Chile. Onces snacks featuring fruit are always popular. Some of these fruits, like figs, strawberries, cherries, peaches, apples, and grapes, are familiar to North Americans, while others are less recognizable. For example, lúcumas (LOO-cu-mahs) look somewhat like kiwis and taste like butterscotch. Chiri-

Chirimoyas are an admired Chilean treat. The fruit has a pear-like flavor and is often served bathed in orange juice and sugar.

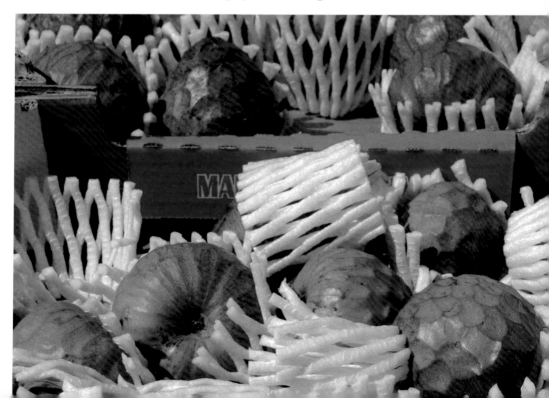

Manjar Banana Smoothie

Two popular Chilean treats, manjar and fruit, combine to make this delicious drink. Dulce de leche (the Spanish term for manjar) can typically be found in the international section of North American grocery stores.

Ingredients
⅓ cup dulce de leche
1 cup milk
1 ripe banana,
    cut in chunks
1 cup ice cubes

Directions
Put all the ingredients in a
    blender. Mix until it is smooth
Serves 2.

Manjar and fruit–two popular Chilean treats–combine to make a delicious banana drink.

moyas (chee-ree-MOH-yas), or custard apples, have a pear-like flavor and an exotic fragrance. They are often served bathed in orange juice and sugar.

Chilean cooks turn these and other fruits into puddings, ice cream, and pastries. Kuchen (KOO-ken), a pie-like pastry filled with fruit and topped with a layer of sweet crumbs, is wildly popular. Kuchen is the German word for cake. Many German immigrants settled in southern Chile in the 1850s. They brought the pastry to Chile. Many southern Chilean towns reflect the German people's influence, as does the popularity of apple, strawberry, and walnut kuchens throughout Chile. According to author and chef, Barbara Hansen, "You don't need to seek out German restaurants or go south to find it [kuchen]. Cafés anywhere may have it just as scones and Danish turn up in coffee shops all over the United States."[14]

Fruits are also turned into delightful beverages. Mote con huesillos (MOH-tay con oo-ay-SEE-yos) is a national favorite that Chileans have been drinking for thousands of years. It is made with dried peaches, cooked wheat kernels, and sugar water. The ingredients are refrigerated until they are icy cold. Then, they are combined in a tall chilled glass and served with a long spoon, much like an ice cream soda.

Sold by street vendors, at roadside stands, and in fancy restaurants, mote con huesillos is a perfect thirst quencher on a hot day. And, it is loaded with vitamins and minerals. It is, says Ruth Van Waerebeek-Gonzalez, "one of the most refreshing, nutritious and healthiest snacks I have come across."[15]

Whether it is a refreshing glass of mote con huesillos, German kuchen, manjar-filled pastries, or a towering sandwich, Chileans like their onces snacks. With so many sweet and savory choices, it would be difficult not to enjoy this evening ritual.

Chapter 4

Holidays and Fiestas

Chileans are social people. Getting together with friends and family over special foods makes any event a celebration. Holidays and special occasions are especially joyful.

Fiestas Patrias

September 18th is Chilean Independence Day. It marks the day in 1810 that the Chilean people began an eight-year fight for independence from Spain. To mark their independence, Chileans celebrate for a full week with **fiestas patrias** (fee-AYS-tas PAH-tree-as), or patriotic parties, that include parades, fireworks, kite flying, dance competitions, rodeos, and lots and lots of traditional food. "The fiestas patrias," according to Joe

Chileans are social people, especially around holidays and special occasions. Fiestas patrias (patriotic parties) include fireworks, lots of food, parades, and rodeos.

"Pepe" Rawlinson, who spent two years in Chile, "are a time for all Chileans to gather together and celebrate their country, culture, and independence. Celebrations of all things Chilean center on their independence day."[16]

A lot of the merrymaking takes place in **fondas** (FONE-dahs), open-air structures with roofs made from tree branches that are set up all over the country. **Empanadas** (em-pah-NAH-das), delicious stuffed pastries that Chileans eat year-round as an appetizer or light meal, are always part of the celebration. "I always associate the special scent of ... the aromatic pino [filling] with the nearing of ... Chilean Independence

Empanadas (pictured) are delicious stuffed pastries that are a source of national pride in Chile.

Day,"[17] explains Liz Caskey, a chef who lives in Chile.

Empanadas look like little stuffed squares or half-moons. They are quite portable and can be eaten on the run. In fact, they are one of the few foods that Chileans eat with their hands. Empanadas probably originated in Spain. The name comes from the Spanish word *empanar*, which means to wrap food in bread dough. Almost every country in Latin America has its own version of the pastry. Chilean empanadas start with tasty bread dough. It is filled with a moist and juicy filling of fish, seafood, chicken, onion, cheese, or pino, which is the most popular. It is the same sweet-salty filling that is used in pastel de choclo. Whatever the choice of filling, it must be moist. The moisture keeps the pastry

Fun Facts About Chile

- Chile is the longest and narrowest country in the world.
- Chile is the 38th largest country in the world.
- Chile's currency is the peso.
- Spanish is the official language.
- Chile's flag is red, white, and blue. It contains one white star.
- Chile's number one export is copper.
- Chile is the world's second largest producer of salmon.
- Chile has a 95.7 percent literacy rate. Students attend school for fourteen years.
- Chile and Ecuador are the only countries in South America that do not border Brazil.
- Chile has more than 2,000 volcanoes. Fifty are active.
- Chilean Patagonia is one of the most environmentally pure places on Earth.
- Some of the best ski centers in the southern hemisphere are found in Chile.
- Chilean rivers are well-known white-water rafting sites.
- Kite flying is a popular Chilean pastime.

from drying out.

Once the empanada is filled, the cook folds the dough over the filling and seals the empanada before it is cooked. Traditionally, empanadas are baked in a

Cowboys and Rodeos

Huasos (oo-AH-sos) are Chilean cowboys. They work on ranches in central and southern Chile. Chilean huasos are admired throughout the country for their horsemanship. Rodeo is the second most popular sport in Chile. Soccer is the first.

Many rodeos are held during fiestas patrias. Unlike North American rodeos that feature roping and bull riding, Chilean rodeos focus on horsemanship. Working in pairs, huasos gallop sideways around a half-moon-shaped ring, herding calves into a designated area. Then, they separate one calf from the herd and pin down that calf against a huge cushion. The cowboys get points for the way they treat the cattle, their horsemanship, and for their costumes, which typically include large sombreros (sohm-BRAIR-ohs) or hats, short jackets with silver buttons, and/or brightly colored triangular capes called ponchos.

Large parties with food and dancing are held after the rodeo.

wood-fired oven similar to a pizza oven. They can also be fried, or baked in a traditional oven. No matter what method is used, the savory pastries are a source of national pride in Chile. "No holiday … would be complete without enjoying a few empanadas! The empanada is to Chile what the hamburger is to the United States,"[18] says Van Waerebeek-Gonzalez.

Asados

Asados (ah-SAH-does), or barbecues, are another part of the fiesta patrias celebrations. They are also a favorite way for Chileans to mark any social occasion.

Chilean asados (barbeques) are known for their huge quantity, variety, and quality of meat.

Chilean barbecue grills are different from those in the United States. Typically, Chilean grills are made from large oil drums that are slit down the middle and mounted on iron legs. A charcoal fire is lit inside the oil drum and a large grate is placed on the top.

Meat is cooked on the grate. And, there is always a lot of it. Steaks, burgers, sausages, chicken, and pork are all likely to be on the menu. Chilean asados are known for the huge quantity and variety of meat that is served, as well as for the meat's good taste and high quality.

Chilean cattle are **free-range**, which means the animals roam freely and feed on natural grasses rather than grain. The meat is leaner and contains less fat and cholesterol than American beef. And, since the animals are not fed any drugs or chemicals, the meat is all-natural.

Asados are often all-day affairs. Chileans insist that grilling is a man's job. The cook is almost always the man of the house. Usually all the men in the family, as well as male friends and neighbors, gather around the barbeque to watch the meat as it cooks. This gathering is actually the start of the party since the men snack, drink, and visit throughout the day. The women make a variety of salads to go with the meat, including Chilean salad. This simple salad made with fresh, ripe tomatoes, onions, hot peppers, olive oil, and cilantro is the most popular of all Chilean salads. Potato salad, corn, tomato, and onion salad, soft-cheese salad, and bean salad are other likely accompaniments.

The meal is eaten in intervals. The cook cuts off pieces of meat for the guests to snack on as it grills. Once the meat is done, everyone has some. Then, the guests visit with each other until they start feeling hungry again. Meanwhile, the cook grills a different variety of meat and the cycle keeps repeating until all the meat is gone.

Doris Hamilton, a writer and teacher who lives in Chile, explains:

> Whenever the weather is nice, even when it isn't, people get together with friends and family, make a fire on the grill, and cook beefsteak, pork chops, sausages, chicken, and whatever else seems to be good to eat that

Chilean Salad

This may be the Chilean people's favorite salad. It is easy to make. Soaking the onions in sugar water removes any bitterness.

Ingredients

1 red onion
2 big tomatoes, sliced into thin rings
1 tablespoon chopped jalapeño pepper
1 tablespoon chopped cilantro
3 tablespoons olive oil
1 teaspoon sugar
salt and pepper to taste

Directions

1. Put the onions in a bowl. Cover with water mixed with the sugar. Let the mixture soak for 10 minutes.
2. Remove the onions from the water. Squeeze the onions to remove the moisture.
3. Mix the tomatoes, onions, cilantro, jalapeño, olive oil, salt and pepper to taste.

Serves 4.

The simple Chilean salad is a likely accompaniment at many asados.

day. The whole preparation of the asado is kind of a ritual, with the men standing around the fire, chatting, laughing, and preparing

Pan de Pascua

There are lots of different recipes for Chilean Christmas bread. Some use yeast and liquor, while others do not. The bread is not difficult to make, but it does use many ingredients. Ground cloves can be substituted for anise seeds.

Ingredients
2 ½ cups flour
3 eggs
1 tablespoon white vinegar
⅓ cup apple juice
½ cup (one stick) butter, warmed
1 ½ teaspoons baking soda
½ cup brown sugar
½ cup white sugar
½ cup raisins
½ cup candied fruit
½ cup chopped walnuts
1 teaspoon cinnamon
1 teaspoon ginger
¼ teaspoon anise seeds
pinch of salt

the barbecue. Meanwhile, the women put together the accompanying salads and set out the dishes, and the children play outside with their cousins and friends. ... The asado is a standard Chilean social event and most people fully enjoy its simplicity as well as its wealth of good eating.[19]

Directions

1. Preheat oven to 300 degrees. Spray a loaf or round pan with nonstick cooking spray.
2. Mix the sugar, butter, and eggs together until creamy. Add the salt, spices, flour, raisins, fruit, nuts, baking powder, vinegar, and apple juice. Mix until you have a thick, moist batter.
3. Pour the batter into the pan. Bake for about 1 hour, until a fork inserted into the center of the bread comes out clean.

Serves 8–12.

It is tradition to end the Chilean Christmas meal with Pan de Pascua.

Christmas Bread

Christmas is another happy time in Chile. Since Chile is in the southern hemisphere, Christmas falls during the summer. Although the weather is hot, Chileans celebrate Christmas in much the same way as people in colder climates do—with Old Man Christmas, the Chilean version of Santa Claus, Christmas trees decorated with white cotton "snow," lots of presents, and a huge dinner on Christmas Eve.

Although menus differ, a typical meal is likely to feature avocados stuffed with crab, roast turkey, and various salads. But no matter what else is served, it is traditional to end the meal with **pan de pascua** (pahn day PAHS-koo-ah), Chilean Christmas bread. The name might confuse Spanish speakers, since the word *pascua* refers to Easter in many Spanish-speaking countries. In Chile, it refers to both Christmas and Easter.

This moist cake-like bread is laced with candied and dried fruit, nuts, and aromatic spices, such as ginger, cinnamon, and anise, an herb that tastes and smells like black licorice. The bread often contains a little bit of rum or brandy, alcoholic beverages that help moisten the pastry.

Many countries throughout the world make similar Christmas breads and cakes. Pan de pascua is quite similar to German stollen (SHTOH-luhn), or German Christmas cake. Chile's German population brought it to their new home, where local cooks adapted the recipe to make it, according to Joelson, "a longtime Chilean treasure."[20]

One change Chilean bakers made was substituting **chancaca** (chan-CAH-ca) for white sugar. Chancaca is a type of hard brown sugar produced in South America. Chilean cooks dissolve it in water. This produces a molasses-like syrup that sweetens the bread and turns it a deep-brown color.

The end result is rich, dense, sweet bread that smells like fruit, sugar, and spices and tastes delicious. Combined with a cup of cola de mono (CO-la day MOH-no), or monkey's tail, a traditional Chilean Christmas drink that is similar to eggnog; it is a perfect treat after Christmas dinner.

Whether as an ending to a holiday meal, the main dish, or a festive snack, special foods like pan de pascua, empanadas, and grilled meats mean it is time to celebrate in Chile. Add in friends and family, and Chileans have a recipe for fun.

Metric conversions

Mass (weight)

1 ounce (oz.)	= 28.0 grams (g)
8 ounces	= 227.0 grams
1 pound (lb.) or 16 ounces	= 0.45 kilograms (kg)
2.2 pounds	= 1.0 kilogram

Liquid Volume

1 teaspoon (tsp.)	= 5.0 milliliters (ml)
1 tablespoon (tbsp.)	= 15.0 milliliters
1 fluid ounce (oz.)	= 30.0 milliliters
1 cup (c.)	= 240 milliliters
1 pint (pt.)	= 480 milliliters
1 quart (qt.)	= 0.96 liters (l)
1 gallon (gal.)	= 3.84 liters

Pan Sizes

8-inch cake pan	= 20 x 4-centimeter cake pan
9-inch cake pan	= 23 x 3.5-centimeter cake pan
11 x 7-inch baking pan	= 28 x 18-centimeter baking pan
13 x 9-inch baking pan	= 32.5 x 23-centimeter baking pan
9 x 5-inch loaf pan	= 23 x 13-centimeter loaf pan
2-quart casserole	= 2-liter casserole

Temperature

212°F	= 100°C (boiling point of water)
225°F	= 110°C
250°F	= 120°C
275°F	= 135°C
300°F	= 150°C
325°F	= 160°C
350°F	= 180°C
375°F	= 190°C
400°F	= 200°C

Length

¼ inch (in.)	= 0.6 centimeters (cm)
½ inch	= 1.25 centimeters
1 inch	= 2.5 centimeters

Notes

Chapter 1: A Land of Plenty

1. Quoted in David Lansing, "Serving Up Santiago," October 29, 2009, enRoute. http://enroute.aircanada.com/en/articles/serving-up-santiago/.

2. Quoted in Beth Pacunas, Tracy Morgan, *Andrew Zimmern Bizarre Foods: Chile*, 2008, The Travel Channel.

3. Daniel Joelson, *Tasting Chile*. New York: Hippocrene, 2004, p. 12.

4. Susan Kohen, telephone interview with the author, March 24, 2010.

5. Ruth Van Waerebeek-Gonzalez, *The Chilean Kitchen*. New York: HP, 1999, p. 228.

Chapter 2: A Cultural Exchange

6. Van Waerebeek-Gonzalez, *The Chilean Kitchen*, p. 130.

7. Quoted in Joelson, *Tasting Chile*, p. 135.

8. Cecilia Fernandez, "Reclaiming Our Own Flavors," December 2001, Nuestro.cl. www.nuestro.cl/eng/stories/people/bocadostipicos.htm..

Chapter 3: Tea Time

9. Kohen, telephone interview with the author.

10. Margaret Snook, "Sanguches," December 3, 2008, Cachando Chile. www.cachandochile.wordpress.com/2008/12/03/sanguches/.

11. Anthony Bourdain, *No Reservations: Chile*, January 2009, The Travel Channel.

12. Quoted in Beth Pacunas, Tracy Morgan, *Andrew Zimmern Bizarre Foods: Chile*, 2008.

13. Joelson, *Tasting Chile*, p. 197.

14. Barbara Hansen, "Coffee and Kuchen in Chile," June 6, 2008, Table Conversation.com. www.tableconversation.com/2008/06/coffee-and-kuch.html.

15. Van Waerebeek-Gonzalez, *The Chilean Kitchen*, p. 276.

Chapter 4: Holidays and Fiestas

16. Joe "Pepe" Rawlinson, "Chile's Independence Day (Fiestas Patrias)," Pepes Chile. http://joeskitchen.com/chile/culture/fiestaspatrias.htm.

17. Liz Caskey, "Bienvenidos September and Empanada Mania," September 2, 2009, Eat Wine. http://eatwineblog.com/2009/09/02/bienvenido-september-and-empanada-mania/.

18. Van Waerebeek-Gonzalez, *The Chilean Kitchen*, p. 16.

19. Doris Hamilton, "Deiciocho: Chile's Month-Long Independence 'Day,'" World and I. www.worldandi.com/subscribers/feature_detail.asp?num=25181.

20. Joelson, *Tasting Chile*, p. 187.

Glossary

asados: Chilean barbecue parties.

caldillo de congrio: Chilean fish chowder.

chancaca: Hard brown sugar.

completos: Large Chilean hotdogs served with multiple toppings.

conquistadors: Spanish explorers who came to the Americas seeking gold and riches.

curanto: A Chilean clambake in which seafood is cooked in a pit filled with hot stones.

empanadas: A type of turnover filled with meat or seafood.

fiestas patrias: Parties that celebrate Chilean Independence Day.

fondas: Temporary open-air buildings that have roofs made of twigs.

free-range: A term used to describe livestock that is not kept penned up.

guanaco: A wild animal similar to a llama.

huasos: Chilean cowboys.

manjar: A sweet made with milk and sugar that tastes like caramel.

Mapuche: Chilean native people who were never conquered by the Spanish.

Moors: North African people who occupied Spain.

onces: Chilean tea time.

pan de pascua: Sweet bread eaten on Christmas Eve in Chile.

pastel de choclo: A savory corn pie.

picadas: Small casual eateries.

pino: A mixture of ground beef, onions, and spices.

Books

Michael Burgan, *Chile*. New York: Children's Press, 2009. Covers Chile's history, geography, economics, and culture with many pictures.

Michael Capek, *Easter Island*. Minneapolis: Twenty-First Century, 2008. Interesting facts about this mysterious island that is part of Chile and its famous statues.

Francesca Davis Dipiazza, *Chile in Pictures*. Minneapolis: Twenty-First Century, 2007. Looks at Chilean history, government, landforms, economics, people, and culture, with lots of color photos and a timeline.

Dana Meachen Rau, *Chile*. New York: Benchmark, 2006. Focuses on Chile's people and culture.

Web Sites

Central Intelligence Agency, "The World Factbook—Chile," (www.cia.gov/library/publications/the-world-factbook/geos/ci.html). Information about Chile's government, economy, people, and geography with a map, flag, and pictures.

Kids Konnect.com, "Chile," (www.kidskonnect.com/subject-index/26-countriesplaces/306-chile.html).

Facts about Chile with lots of links to maps, photos, and information about Easter Island, Chilean holidays, and food.

Time for Kids, "Chile" (www.timeforkids.com/TFK/kids/hh/goplaces/article/0,28376,1113759,00.html). Provides fast facts about Chile, a timeline, sightseeing guide, and an e-postcard.

Whats4Eats, "Chile: Recipes and Cuisine," (www.whats4eats.com/south-america/chile-cuisine). Information about Chilean food with pictures and links to recipes.

Index

Picture Credits

Cover Photo: © Emilio Ereza/Alamy

© Krys Bailey/Alamy, 19

© Trevor Brooke/Alamy, 11

© Bon Appetit/Alamy, 18, 35, 38, 49

© Danita Delimont/Alamy, 42

EPD Photos, 32

© Emilio Ereza/Alamy, 26–27

© FoodPix/Jupiterimages/Getty Images, 30

© David R. Frazier Photolibrary, Inc./Alamy, 7

Gale/Cengage Learning, 5

© Gastromedia/Alamy, 47

© imagebroker/Alamy, 37

© John Warburton-Lee Photography/Alamy, 14

© Tracey Kusiewicz/Foodie Photography/Getty
  Images, 36

© Lonely Planet Images/Alamy, 24

© M. Timothy O'Keefe/Alamy, 45

© Robert Harding Picture Library Ltd/Alamy, 41

© Rick Souders/FoodPix/Getty Images, 23

© Michael Sparrow/Alamy, 21

© Ryan B. Stevenson/Alamy, 9

About the Author

Barbara Sheen is the author of more than 60 books for young people. She lives with her family in New Mexico. In her spare time, she likes to swim, walk, garden, and read. Of course she loves to cook!